Promises for the Battle

+———+

Douglas W. Knighton

Copyright © 2007 by Douglas W. Knighton

Promises for the Battle
by Douglas W. Knighton

Printed in the United States of America

ISBN-13: 978-1-60034-932-4
ISBN-10: 1-60034-932-3

All rights reserved solely by the author. The author guarantees all contents are original and do not infringe upon the legal rights of any other person or work. No part of this book may be reproduced in any form without the permission of the author. The views expressed in this book are not necessarily those of the publisher.

Unless otherwise indicated, scripture references are the author's translation. All other Scripture references are taken from *New American Standard Bible* (NASB). Copyright © 1960, 1977, 1995 by the Lockman Foundation.

www.xulonpress.com

Table of Contents

Introduction vii

Success 11

Integrity 29

Perseverance 47

Courage 65

Forgiveness 83

Freedom 101

Thinking 119

Patience 137

Help 155

Speech 173

About the Author 191

Scripture Index 193

Introduction

When the Israeli shepherd who would one day become King David first went to war, he faced an unusual situation. He understood he must respond to the enemy's challenge because the honor of the God he worshiped was at stake. He understood that the consequences of success would be a secure and happy future. He also understood that he needed the right weapon system to defeat his foe. Someone offered him his battle gear, but it didn't fit and he hadn't trained with it. So David took inventory of the weapons available to him and chose the ones that would enable him to face and defeat his enemy.

Fighting the "fight of faith" is not optional for us. We must all battle against attitudes of unbelief as we become aware of them in our hearts. We will even benefit by making peremptory strikes to destroy any thought pattern that could turn into unbelief. Where specific actions do not spring from just one sinful concept, we can battle the behavior. To fight this fight effectively we need the right weapons. David's staff and sling were right for his struggle. The rifle is an indispensable weapon to an infantryman as he fights for freedom and justice. The scalpel is an indispensable weapon to a surgeon battling disease. "The Sword of the Spirit, which is the Word of God," is the indispensable weapon we must wield to keep our hearts free so we can experience the "unfathomable riches" of the grace of Christ, both now and in the age to come.

Promises are particularly effective portions of God's Word for defeating attitudes and actions of unbelief, for faith looks forward to promises. Faith is confidence about a promised future, growing out of evidence from the past that the one who made the promise can and will keep it. So the Word of God presents God's promises. It presents evidence he can and will keep his promises. It presents instructions for how to live in order to obtain what was promised. This book is designed to help us successfully fight to maintain our faith in God by "slinging" promise-pebbles at every instance of unbelief.

God's promises come in several forms. Sometimes they are straightforward: Here's what I will do for you! Sometimes they are in the form of conditions: If you will ... , I will ... . Often promises come in the form of commands, because embedded in the command is the implication that what God is telling us to do is what is best for us. Similarly wisdom aphorisms present us with truth about life that imply happiness will attend us if we align our lives with these truths. Commands and aphorisms are simply camouflaged conditional promises.

So each of the chapters that follow presents a series of promises, in one form or another. These promises are suited to help us fight to maintain our faith in specific challenging periods of life. Each chapter will contain seven biblical texts, followed by a brief comment and prayer. The comments are not meant to be exhaustive (or exhausting). They are meant to stimulate our faith by making us think about the goodness of God and the glory of his grace. So a page will always be provided for you to write down any observations or ideas that will help you make my words more significant to you. Each chapter will also contain one Scripture text followed by a prayer of praise. For it is fitting that we not only appropriate God's promised grace, but also that we tell him how much we delight in this particular facet of his holiness.

Success

Paralysis is not always a physical condition. Sometimes we are paralyzed by fear, particularly when we encounter challenging new situations. Looking at ourselves and acknowledging our peculiar inadequacies, our confidence plummets. But success in our endeavors does not ultimately rest in us. It rests in God's will and determination to make us successful. Meditating on the promises that follow will help us defeat the unbelief that makes us afraid to try, and will empower us to move forward with faith.

Gracious Success

A warrior is not delivered by great strength. A horse is a false hope for victory. ... Behold, the eye of the Eternal is on those who fear him, on those who hope for his lovingkindness. *Psalm 33:16-18*

Strong and valiant warriors went down to glorious defeat at Thermopylae. Courageous and well-trained horses were not enough for Lee's cavalry at Gettysburg. The strength and courage of the Spartans had served them well in dozens of other battles. J.E.B. Stuart's horses drove the Union army crazy for months. But success is not ultimately dependent on a soldier's equipment or the quality of his training or on his psychological or physical strength. God is sovereign over human affairs. Sometimes he works in ways we cannot see or understand. But often he acts in response to the relationship he has with his people. In so far as it depends on us, success comes to those who fear and hope in God. Fear keeps us from acting contrary to God's requirements for justice, because we know the consequences for disobedience. Hope for his grace honors his ability and intention to do more good than we could ever ask or expect. Because God wants us to appreciate the fullness of his glory, he works for people who are totally open to his involvement in their projects.

> Father, my heart is completely yours. Let your gracious strength be shown perfectly in and through my humble weaknesses. Amen.

Gracious Success

The Measure of Success

I shall continue with you all for your progress and joy in the faith, so that your boasting may abound in Christ Jesus. *Philippians 1:25-26*

Abundant boasting! More and more: more talk of how gracious, generous, faithful, practical, timely, appropriate, surprising, and useful Jesus has been toward us. More and more: more immediate, frequent, and exuberant; more accurate, bold, reverent, and personal praise for "mercy and well-timed grace." Untiring, unending, and unobjectionable testimony. Faith is not complete until boasting occurs, because praise affirms both the receipt and the recognition of Jesus' glorious gifts. Paul chose to live and create such boasting; we can have a similar priority. We also can choose to continue to minister in ways that cause people to progress in their faith and experience an increase in the enjoyment of the way Jesus comes through for them every day. What a joy! What a challenge! For we can help others progress only if we are progressing. When the result of our daily confidence abounds in boasting, then we can work for the same pattern in others. This promise keeps us going: when others progress and find joy in their faith, boasting in Jesus will abound.

> O Lord, grant me Paul's maturity in the face of every trial, Paul's patience with those I serve, and Paul's joy as I experience success. Amen.

Promises for the Battle

The Measure of Success

The Means of Success

> These instructions shall not depart from your mouth, but you shall meditate on them day and night, so that you may be careful to do according to all that is written; for then you will make your way prosperous and have success. *Joshua 1:8*

We pay attention to the last words of great people, especially if they are old. Moses was old when he talked to Joshua for the last time. He had nothing to gain by Joshua's obedience. He had no hidden agenda. Committed together to the same vision for years, they were partners; committed to the same mission, they were comrades. But Moses' words were not just for his protégé; they were for all of us. The promise can be summarized this way: You must *be* before you can *do*, and do before you can *have*. God knows that our minds shape our behavior, and our behaviors shape our destiny. When our minds are filled with the promises of God concerning how loving, powerful, wise, timely, and reliable he is, we will trust all of his instructions about how to relate to people, some of whom do not always live righteously or justly. Diligent repetition and study of God's operations order will create a reservoir of wisdom from which we can draw as we consider the thousands of choices that decide the success of our journey.

> Lord Jesus, renew my mind as I review your instructions every day, and fulfill every good desire and the work of faith with power. Amen.

Promises for the Battle

The Means of Success

Humble Success

+——+

> Jesus took a towel ... and began to wash the disciples' feet. ... He said to Peter, "If I do not wash you, you have no part with me." *John 13: 4-8*

Jesus presents himself as both Teacher and Lord, full of wisdom and power to provide all his followers need. He is intimate with the Father, having all resources in his control and immediate access to those resources. And Jesus knows his students; he knows that even though he has cleansed our hearts from their former desires and loyalties, we need to be kept clean. So he becomes at once a model and a teacher of humility and service. By requiring Peter to receive and to emulate the foot washing process, Jesus inspires us to do the same. When we allow another disciple to serve us out of the resources and wisdom Jesus supplies, we humbly confirm our own need for his grace. At the same time, our hearts are washed of the desires and loyalties that tend to accumulate from our daily interaction with others. When we humbly serve other disciples as Jesus did, we experience a renewed connection with him and a confidence that we will always have more than enough grace for ourselves and for others.

> Father, open my eyes so I may see the feet that need washing all around me. Open my heart so I will receive "water and soap" from my friends that will help me live. Amen.

Humble Success

Perfected Success

✧

He who began a good work in you will perfect it. ... your love will abound still more and more in real knowledge and all discernment, so that you may approve the things that are excellent, in order to be sincere and blameless going into the day of Christ. Philippians 1:6-10

If one of the keys to success is to "begin with the end in view," one way to measure current success is to look forward to the day from which we will look back on everything. This method helps us gauge our success, because it allows us to compare how we are to how we want to be. Another approach is to look inside ourselves. This method helps us by illuminating how much we've grown emotionally and intellectually. A third approach is to observe and evaluate our choices. The most concrete of the three, this method keeps us from fooling ourselves, because action always follows approval; when we approve and choose what is excellent, we are becoming successful. Our success at the coming of Christ — our consistency and irreproachability — are contingent on how well we are able to love and choose. Fortunately our contingency is God's certainty. As often as we fail to finish good work that we've begun, God never fails. He will complete his work in us: perfecting our affections, our actions, and our acceptance.

> God of majesty and mystery, work in me so I will and do all that pleases you and profits me, both now and for eternity. Amen.

Promises for the Battle

Perfected Success

Success' Secret

> I have learned to be content in every circumstance. I know how to get along with humble means, and I also know how to live in prosperity; I have learned the secret:... I can do all things through him who strengthens me. *Philippians 4:12-13*

Success is not measured by the contingencies of the journey. When Paul was stoned or beaten or shipwrecked or starving, he could not see those experiences as evidence of failure in his mission to take the Gospel to the nations. When Paul was well received, praised, honored, fed and sheltered, he could not say that he was being successful. For the circumstances surrounding the delivery and reception of the truth of Christ couldn't tell him anything about the overall effect the message was having in the community. He learned to be content in both positive and negative circumstances. So can we. Like the apostle, we can focus on the mission and on the Master. Whether it's evangelism or some other purpose toward which we work, if we teach ourselves to see the work through the lens of the goal, we'll be able to shrug off the distractions we encounter. If we teach ourselves to rely on the presence and providence of Jesus, we'll gain the inner strength necessary to pull our feet out of the muck and take the next step.

> Lord, no matter what the facts, grant me confidence in you and a clear dream, so I will have power in the present and success in the end.

Success' Secret

Wise Success

+———+

> If the axe is dull and he does not sharpen its edge, then he must use more strength. Wisdom has the advantage of giving success. *Ecclesiastes 10:10* (NASB)

Success involves completing all the steps of a process that lead to the outcome we desire, so that when we achieve our goal, we are able to enjoy our destination. We can chop down trees with a dull axe, but that will be all we accomplish. If it takes two or three times as long as it might with a sharp axe, and if we're so exhausted or — worse — disinterested when we finish, then we are not successful. The limited success of the first marathon runner was lauded but not copied. Sharpening the axe is an act of faith. We are trusting the Lord's wisdom that time spent preparing to cut will yield more and better results. We are believing the implication that having energy to enjoy the fruit of our labor is part of his design. We are believing that the God who works smarter rather than harder wants us to imitate him. Continuous preparation of this nature carries over into every area of life: Study on a seat makes it easier to think on our feet. Regularly reviewing the good and attractive qualities of our mates makes it easier to remain faithful during temptation.

> O Lord, grant me the humility necessary to admit the need to change what I'm doing, and the foresight to see how advantageous change is.

Wise Success

Successful Praise

✝━━━✝

God saw all that he had made, and behold, it was very good. ...God blessed the seventh day and sanctified it, because in it he rested from all his work which God had created. *Genesis 1:31; 2:3* (NASB)

O God our Creator, we work in your rest. Because you were satisfied with all that you had done, we are able to do. Because you succeeded, we can pursue success in every area of our lives. Fitting all the pieces precisely was "very good." Now we are confident of a stable and reasonable environment in which to work out what it means to be created in your image. Oh, that seventh day is so very valuable to us! And even more we value the first day of the week. For you sanctified that day by finishing an even greater work, by creating a more magnificent success. You delivered up your Son because of our sin, and raised him because of our justification. You overcame every obstacle to your plan. The nothing of pre-existence did not stop you, and the hideousness of our sin did not deter you, from realizing the accomplishment of your dream. Now as you work for those who wait for you, the final goal comes into view. Daily you sanctify every child and draw us closer to the time when we will be able to experience the fullness of what you created us to know: the wonder of your glory seen through the millions of kindnesses that come to us through Jesus Christ our Lord. Amen.

Promises for the Battle

Successful Praise

Integrity

+———+

Being "double-minded" makes us unstable in all our ways. Whether the divide is spiritual, ethical, moral, intellectual, or emotional, always having our hearts at a fork in the road causes much unhappiness and often leads to regret. The single-minded person — the person of integrity — however, experiences no such inner turmoil. Rather, integrity creates a sense of wholeness and peace. To encourage us to defeat our unbelieving inclinations to serve more than one master, God offers wonderful benefits to us if we will maintain our integrity.

Satisfying Integrity

✢━━━✢

> You can not serve two masters; for either you will hate the one and love the other, or you will hold to one and despise the other. You cannot serve God and mammon. ... So seek first his kingdom and his righteousness; and all these things shall be added to you.
> *Matthew 6:24, 33*

A wise man once said, "What we hope in, we worship; what we worship, we serve." So there is a sense in which everyone lives with integrity. At any one time we can only have **one** source of hope. Our eggs are always in one basket or another, even if we change baskets frequently. Jesus simply says that if we hook up with God, we will be far more satisfied in life than if we serve some created entity. For serving mammon means we must secure and protect and nurture and manipulate it, while serving God means placing ourselves in a position for him to work for us: "There is no other god like ours, who works for those who wait for him." The choice is simple: the created or the Creator. Such is Jesus' promise: If we seek to live under God's rule and by God's rules, we will receive God's rewards. This is integrity worth maintaining, worth fighting for.

> "Behold, as the eyes of servants look to the hand of their master, as the eyes of a maid to the hand of her mistress; so my eyes look to you O Eternal, my God, until you are gracious to me." Amen.

Promises for the Battle

Satisfying Integrity

Abiding Integrity

✦————✦

O Eternal, who may abide in your tent? Who may dwell on your holy hill? The one who walks with integrity, and works righteousness, and speaks truth in his heart.
Psalm 15:1-2

David's three conditions for fellowship with the Creator may seem stringent at first glance. But when we pause to think about them, they are more than reasonable. For no other kind of person would enjoy being with him. Deceptive, depraved, dissemblers would be utterly uncomfortable in God's presence, for they have nothing in common with him. Absolutely loyal commitment is the first of God's requirements here, just as it is first in the Ten Commandments. This is part of what it means to "walk with integrity." God wants people whose hearts are completely his, for he himself finds full delight in who he is. Since God is the center of his own purposes in creation, he must be the center of our purposes, or we will not abide in his presence. The One moving his people from the slums of self-centeredness into the palaces of his glory, asks that we stay on the road with him, intent on reaching our destination, continually reminding ourselves of the goodness that awaits us.

> Glorious King, grant me a clearer vision of the wonder and joy of your "holy hill," so I will not look back to the wretchedness of the "Sodom" I have left behind. Strengthen my heart along the way to glory with Jesus.

Abiding Integrity

Fearless Integrity

✝———✝

The one who walks in integrity walks securely. But those who pervert their ways will be found out. *Proverbs 10:9*

The military profession rests on the concept of integrity. Subordinates assume their leaders will have integrity before they commit themselves to follow their lead. To our servicemen the leader's integrity implies two commitments: first, a commitment to work for their good — especially to create an environment that makes mission accomplishment possible — and second, a commitment to do what is right. If this good is not the end toward which leaders aim, they are not living with integrity, and they can't hide this fact for long. If doing right is not the way they achieve this end, someone will find out. Certainly, God always knows. Eventually the fabric of deception will fall apart and they will be left standing naked before the world. But through integrity we need never live in fear that someone will dig the skeletons out of our closets, for peace of mind is its reward. Security is the companion of those who walk according to their confidence in the goodness and wisdom of God, never yielding to the temptation of expediency.

> "Guard my soul and deliver me, O God. Do not let me be ashamed, for I take refuge in you. Let integrity and uprightness preserve me, for I wait for you," through Jesus Christ, who loved me to the end. Amen.

Fearless Integrity

Stabilizing Integrity

✢

Equip the saints for the work of service, namely, the building up of the body of Christ until we all attain to the same unity of faith and knowledge as the Son of God — to maturity, to the measure of the stature which belongs to the fullness of Christ — so we won't be ... tossed about by every wind of doctrine devised by clever men. *Ephesians 4:12-13*

Integrity is not just "walking the talk." It is being strong enough internally to stay on the path. Pilots use radio guidance systems and autopilots to keep them on course so they won't wander around among the clouds. Surgeons draw lines on the skin and read the tissue planes so they can cut exactly where they should. Similarly, Christians must encourage one another to attain spiritual integrity, which is the union of faith and knowledge in the heart. When we trust God according to how much we know of God, we have integrity — internal unity: This is maturity. Jesus lived this way; and it is his intent for us as well. So it should be our goal in service to one another. One of the primary benefits of such integrity is the ability to sail through cleverly devised but inaccurate teaching without being capsized. God's promise to us when we gain this integrity is stability of heart and mind.

Father, in knowing Jesus, I know you are wise, powerful, righteous, loving, faithful, good, truthful, gracious, merciful, patient, & forgiving. Unite my faith to this knowledge. Amen.

Stabilizing Integrity

Fruitful Integrity

The seed which fell among the thorns are individuals who have heard the Word, but let the worries and riches and pleasures of this life choke it out, so they produced no mature fruit. But the seed in the good soil are the ones who hear the Word with a noble and good heart, hold it fast, and bear fruit with perseverance. Luke 8:14-15

In this parable Jesus contrasts the honest and good heart of the godly person with the ignoble and reprehensible heart of the merely religious. If we were simply religious, we'd only have a superficial appreciation of the hope and power of Jesus' message. So when we experienced obstacles and/or pleasures that oppose his teaching, we would let go of the good Jesus offered. But if we have a passionate care for, and commitment to, the joys of a covenant relationship with God, Jesus says we have a noble and good heart. This singular focus, this **integrity**, helps us persevere in doing good. When we are whole-hearted in our response to the good news of the kingdom, we will more readily hold fast to the hope laid up for us in heaven, and more readily obey God's commands, especially when faced with competing claims that might divide our hearts. Integrity will make us unlike those who light candles and put them under baskets, but like those whose faith keeps them shining their lights into a dark world.

> Father, I need to listen well to what Jesus has to say. Only he has the words of eternal life. Unite in me a joyful hearing and an eager doing of your whole counsel. Amen.

Fruitful Integrity

Suffering Integrity

+———+

Suffer hardship with me, as a good soldier of Christ Jesus. No soldier in active service entangles himself in the affairs of everyday life, so that he may please the one who enlisted him as a soldier. Also if anyone competes as an athlete, he does not win the prize unless he competes according to the rules. *2 Timothy 2:3-5* (NASB)

The Apostle Paul was able to suffer hardship because of his integrity. The promise that attends this singleness of purpose will sustain us through much pain! Judging from the kind of analogies Paul used, this should be common sense. But evidently we all need reminding. Integrity in this sense involves having one goal and bending every aspect of our lives to attaining it. The value of the goal, and our strong desire for it, motivate us to refuse other opportunities that present themselves; for example, David Brainerd turned down a prestigious pastorate so he could continue working among the Indians in early 18th Century America. The prize also motivates us to submit ourselves to certain behavioral constraints; just as surgeons do when they gown and scrub before surgery, or just as soldiers do when they don all their battle-rattle before a mission. Such integrity will even help us suffer the loss of the good, so we can obtain what is really excellent.

> Lord, with Paul, I pray that my love will abound still more and more in real knowledge and all discernment, so that I may approve the things that are excellent, in order to be sincere and blameless until the end. Amen.

Suffering Integrity

Enlightened Integrity

✦━━━✦

If we say that we have fellowship with God and yet walk in the darkness, we lie and do not practice the truth; but if we walk in the light as he himself is in the light, we have fellowship with one another and the blood of Jesus his Son cleanses us from all sin. *1 John 1:6-7*

One startling analogy the Bible uses for living with integrity is "walking in the light." This involves acknowledging all of reality as God defines it, which gives us panoramic vision rather than tunnel vision. Tunnel vision causes us to love and worship a portion of creation by blowing it out of proportion, so we cannot make wise and loving decisions that take into consideration all necessary factors. Three marvelous benefits accrue to us when we walk in the light: 1) Spiritual cleansing: for seeing all of reality surely involves confessing our sin as God reveals it. 2) Fellowship with one another: instead of living in our own privately defined world, we participate together with everyone whose hope is in the Lord. 3) Fellowship with the fullness of the godhead: when we and God are both "in the light," we are both enjoying the truth that God is the one true source of joy in life. Holding fast to this integrity will give us the strength to face anything, even tragedy.

> Thank you for transferring me from the kingdom of darkness into the kingdom of light; from allegiance to the Prince of Darkness, to the Light of the World. Keep me following the path as you light it. Amen.

Enlightened Integrity

Praises of Integrity

✝━━━✝

God built his sanctuary like the heights, like the earth which he has founded forever. He also chose David his servant, ... to shepherd Jacob his people, and Israel his inheritance. So he shepherded them according to the integrity of his heart, and guided them with his skillful hands. *Psalm 78:69-72* (NASB)

Father, you created for your glory and declared that the knowledge of your glory will fill the earth, as the waters cover the sea. You oversaw the dispersion of the genetic lines of Adam and Eve, so that at the right time Jesus would be born of a virgin to die in the place of your chosen people from every tribe and tongue and nation of earth, to the praise of your glory. You have never wavered in your righteous commitment to display the fullness of your glory. Even our fallible leaders are evidence of your integrity in this matter. In the Trinity there is no division. Father, Son and Holy Spirit rejoice with one joy and work together with one purpose. Jesus came and accomplished your will as though he were at a banquet. By maintaining your own integrity, you have encouraged me to maintain mine. The Spirit now gives me a heart that delights in following your way. He causes me to obey your commands with the same joy Jesus did. He enables me to know the certainty of your promises to those whose way is one with yours. You are indeed the great ONE! Amen.

Praises of Integrity

Perseverance

✝———✝

No one likes a quitter. We especially despise the quitter we sometimes see in the mirror. When we quit, we are not living by faith, for faith in someone implies our willingness to keep believing until the person we trust delivers on the promise. The Lord does not want us to look at quitters in the mirror either. Because gaining eternal life only occurs for those who persevere until the end, God provides many promises specifically intended to promote our perseverance and to annihilate the unbelief that leads us to flee the battlefield in the middle of the fight.

Hopeful Endurance

+———+

Let us exult in our tribulations, knowing that tribulation brings about endurance; and endurance, evidence; and evidence, hope. *Romans 5:3-4*

God uses several means to keep us trusting in him to the end. One of the most frequent is tribulation. He seems to favor it more than other means because faith is like a muscle which only grows stronger as it repeatedly encounters resistance. Tribulation is the resistance our faith needs for it to remain strong enough to be obedient, even unto death. God led Israel through the wilderness to humble them and to test their faith, so he might do good to them in the end. So he warned them to watch out for the good times: "Beware, lest when you have eaten and are satisfied ... then your heart becomes proud, and you forget the Eternal, your God, who brought you from the land of Egypt." Today tribulation forces us to ask the question, "Is Jesus really my source of joy in life?" The more we can answer "Yes" to this question, in spite of our circumstances, the more joy we will actually experience as he brings us through each difficulty. Then our confidence of future good will grow as we see how well he keeps us going.

> Faithful God, help me to see clearly all you are doing to bring me through my troubles, and give me boldness to bless you as I relate to others the hope I have in troubled times. Amen.

Promises for the Battle

Hopeful Endurance

Persevering Sowers

✢

The one who sows to his own flesh shall from the flesh reap corruption, but the one who sows to the Spirit shall from the Spirit reap eternal life. So let us not lose heart in doing good, for in due time we shall reap if we do not give up. *Galatians 6:8-9*

Ranger training was hard! Through the dark nights and bleary-eyed days of classes and field training, our goals hung from a stick and bobbed before our eyes. We set our priorities and ordered our activities so we would obtain the result we desired. The objective hung in full view and kept us going, day after interminable day. In a similar way Paul holds out a carrot to help us obtain our ultimate goal, namely an eternal life of fellowship with God. He also places the pitchfork behind, to keep us from turning in the opposite direction. Without these strong motivations, we would be less likely to do what is necessary for the result that we want. For the metaphorical "sow to the Spirit" translates into the laborious and often exasperating reality of "doing good." The faith that profits us works itself out in loving acts for others at every opportunity, but not always easily. For the joy of eternal life which Jesus set before us, we must, and can, trust him enough to lay down our lives in the service of others.

> Enlighten me, O Lord, to the glories of eternal life with you. And show me that any future I can make for myself is worthless. Then fill me with love that won't let me quit. Amen.

Persevering Sowers

Sympathetic Grace

+——+

> We have a high priest who can sympathize with our weaknesses, One who has been tested according to all the things that test us, yet without sin. Let us therefore draw near with confidence to the throne of grace, that we may receive mercy and may find grace to help in time of need. *Hebrews 4:15-16*

If we would stay true to our commitment to Christ, we must remember that he will help us when our faith is tested. To obtain that help we must approach his throne and ask for what we need independent self-sufficiency is not welcomed in his kingdom. We should feel encouraged to approach him because he knows what we're going through and sympathizes with us: He feels the frustration of having to wait for justice. He feels the annoyance of being misunderstood. He feels fear of anticipated suffering. He experienced all this, yet he never disobeyed his Father in unbelief. So when we come to him for help because we can't seem to keep trusting God's promises to bring about justice at the right time, to reveal the motives of everyone's heart, or to turn our stumbling blocks into stepping stones to joy, he will welcome us, and strengthen our hearts through the ministry of the indwelling Spirit, sympathetically giving us the well-timed grace we need.

> Thank you, Lord Jesus, for going ahead and for turning back to offer me a helping hand. The riches of your grace and the sweetness of your mercy are wonderful and give me hope. Amen.

Sympathetic Grace

Beloved Keeper

+———+

The Eternal is near to all who call upon him in truth. He will fulfill the desire of those who fear him. He will also hear their cry and save them. The Eternal keeps all who love him; but all the wicked, he will destroy. *Psalm 145:18-20*

If we want to be kept by God, we must love him. What could be easier? What could be more enjoyable? How could we not love someone who has the power to generate and sustain himself according to his perfect wisdom? When we consider that this eternal God listens for the cries of those who accept their finitude, so that he can work for our good, will not love arise in our hearts? Shouldn't we readily love the One who will fulfill our desires as we conform ours to his? It only makes sense to love such a God. It also makes sense for him to keep those who love him. For he is most glorified in us when we are most satisfied in him. The more we seek our satisfaction in him, the more his glory is displayed. So he is righteous and just to keep those who love him. On the other hand, the wicked — those who don't love God so that they call upon him for all he can do on their behalf — deserve to be destroyed. For they have committed the most heinous of crimes.

> "O my God, preserve my soul, for I am your godly one. Save your servant who trusts in you. Be gracious to me, O Lord, for to you I cry all day long," in Jesus' name. Amen.

Beloved Keeper

A Heart For The Work

With fear and trembling, work out your salvation; for it is God who is at work in you, so you will purpose and work with the best possible attitude. *Philippians 2:12-13*

Christian life is like a walk along the beach — in water up to our knees. We must concentrate every step we take, so the waves of circumstance don't knock us off our feet. And we must be aware of our attitude. If we are to persevere to the end, "holding fast to the word of life" is imperative. God has placed us in difficult and threatening positions. Therefore we must fear and tremble, so we will not forget the wonderful promises that propelled us into the surf in the first place. Left to ourselves we would soon tire of the shifting sands and the surging sea; we would cease believing he knew the path of life. But God is also working inside our souls so that our desire to finish is strong enough to bring about our long-term obedience. He trains the taste buds of our hearts, so we consume his words with gusto. In the midst of turmoil, he enables us to rise above grudging duty and parochial pressure by causing us to delight in him and in his design for our good.

> Lord Jesus, thank you for enabling me to obey you with a good will. May I humbly hold fast to your word so I neither grumble nor complain. Rather, let my life shine with the light of delight in you and your work. Amen.

A Heart For The Work

Guarded on the Upward Way

†———†

I lift up my eyes to the hills. From whence shall my help come? My help is from the Eternal, who made heaven and earth. He will not allow your foot to slip; he who keeps you will not slumber ... The Eternal will protect you from all evil; he will keep your soul ... from this time forth and forever. Psalm 121:1-8

This "psalm of ascent" was sung by pilgrims on their way **up** to worship on the temple mount. The journey was long and arduous; the hills of Israel were not easy to traverse. So the question easily arose, "How shall we make it up those hills to worship in the presence of the Lord?" As we walk through the valley of the shadow of death and climb the mountains of modernity on our way to worship in the Lord's presence, we ask the same question, and receive the same answer: We cannot make it on our own, but we don't need to worry. For our God seeks those who will truly and passionately worship him. Therefore he watches over us constantly and carefully. He becomes the traction plates on the soles of our souls. No evil will knock us off the mountain path. For we trust in God Almighty, who is God of the living not the dead. Nothing can take us out of his hand.

> Eternal Father, thank you for the strength this promise gives to my weary legs. Cause me to remember with joy the reality of your ever watchful & protecting presence. Amen.

Guarded on the Upward Way

Way Out Endurance

✢

If you think you stand, take heed lest you fall. No test is new or unique; and God is faithful, in that he will not allow you to be tested beyond your ability, but with the test will even provide the way out, that you may be able to endure it. *1 Corinthians 10:12-13*

As the best basketball players move toward the basket, they watch for someone who may be open for a better shot. So in our movement toward Heaven, we must be alert for the way out of situations which present the possibility of obtaining our joy from someone or something other than God. If we will watch for it, we will find it. For Jesus has promised it will be available. God is faithful to his promise to complete the work he began in us. He knows us, and how strong our faith is. He does not ask us to fight temptation. Rather, we must flee it by turning away *from* worshipping any creation that promises us joy, and *toward* worshipping only the Creator. We cannot serve God and mammon. So we must beware, lest in our everyday activities we become idolaters, hoping in our profession, our power, or our possessions for the good that only God gives. "My hope is in the Lord, who gave himself for me." When we crave him, we will not cave in.

> Faithful Lord, I have trusted you with my whole life. Be the lamp to my feet and the light to my path, so I will keep going after you around every obstacle. Amen.

Way Out Endurance

Praised By Perseverance

✝──✝

Blessed be the God and Father of our Lord Jesus Christ, who according to his great mercy has caused us to be born again ... and who protects us by his power through faith for a salvation ready to be revealed in the last time. *1 Peter 1:3-5*

How precious is the hope you have given me, O God. You began a good work in me and you have promised to complete it. You will not withhold your compassion from me; your lovingkindness and your truth will continually preserve me. Nothing can separate me from the love you show me in Christ Jesus, and you have proved this repeatedly. I remember how you kept Abraham and Moses and Joshua and Hannah and David and Isaiah and Habakkuk and Mary and Peter and John and Paul through the difficult days of their lives. What an encouragement their stories are! By your power their faith did not fail. Hoping against hope they rested in you, and you gave them perseverance. How wonderful it is to be part of those for whom Jesus suffered and died, part of all he redeemed from every tribe and tongue and people and nation, who definitely and assuredly will worship you, because those whom he justified, he also glorified. Because I am crucified with Christ according to your will, I can live by faith in him who loved me and gave himself for me forever. Amen.

Praised By Perseverance

Courage

―✛―――✛―

The unbelief of timidity indicates that we are not convinced the Lord is with us or for us. It also signifies that we realize our own inadequacy for meeting the enemy on the spiritual battlefield. While we recognize that courage is necessary, the question we ask is: How do we generate courage in our hearts when we need it most? The answer is to fill our minds with the promises God makes that are specifically designed to increase our boldness in the face of adversity and challenge.

Peaceful Courage

✢

Never be anxious; but in everything, by prayer and by supplication with thanksgiving, let your requests be made known to God. And the peace of God, which overrides every idea, shall keep your hearts and your minds from escaping Christ Jesus. *Philippians 4:6-7*

Winston Churchill's nine word commencement address, "Never give up! Never give up! Never give up!" is possible by the grace of God, as he answers prayer in the face of every attack. Since Jesus' coming is at hand, we should demonstrate forbearance, Paul warns. But the imminence of the physical world, with all its seemingly powerful forces arrayed against God's people, makes this difficult. We are drawn away from the promise of eternal life into the anxiety of temporal existence, the fear of misplaced confidence. The courage to hold fast to Christ comes from the peace we experience in answered prayer. When we humble ourselves in prayer, recognizing God's superiority, and when we present the specifics of our requests with gratitude, God answers. He calms our fears and overpowers any ideas we might have had of forsaking Jesus.

> Almighty God, the world speaks death to me every day. Search my heart and know my anxious thoughts. Show me the truth about your wisdom and power, so I will hold fast the word of life until Jesus returns. Amen.

Peaceful Courage

Courageous Humility

———✢———

Humble yourselves, therefore, under the mighty hand of God, that he may exalt you at the proper time, casting all your anxiety upon him, because he cares for you. *1 Peter 5:6-7*

Hanging on to our anxiety feeds our sense of self-sufficiency and our commitment to self-exaltation. Since pride actually goes before our downfall, clasping our anxiety confirms the truth that the fastest way down is up. But the fastest way to "glory and honor and immortality" is down. Our first act of humility is to confess our need for God to mercifully forgive our sin. Immediately he will exalt us to a position of fellowship, for our justification is of great concern to him. Another act of humility before God is serving his people. To do this in a way that honors our master, we must give up our anxiety about whether or not our needs will be met. Peter tells us two truths about God that will move us to trust him with our worries: 1) God is mighty. He has the power to satisfy his own needs; therefore he has the ability to care for ours. 2) He is concerned about us. Since he did what was necessary to remove the obstacle of our sin, we can trust him to provide for all our needs, especially what we need to serve others.

> Exalted Lord, I am encouraged that what concerns me concerns you. Grant me the grace I need to serve humbly in your name.

Courageous Humility

Fruitful Courage

+———+

Blessed are those who trust in the Eternal and whose trust is the Eternal. For they will be like trees planted by the water, that extend their roots by a stream. They will not fear when the heat comes; rather, their leaves will be green, and they will not be anxious in a year of drought nor cease to yield fruit. *Jeremiah 17:7-8*

Everyone of us wants our life to "count," to be "significant," to have "meaning." Since we have been created in the image of God, and according to his purpose, we must see our significance in those terms. The green leaves and fruit of Jeremiah's analogy are the attitudes and actions which allow people to see clearly the glory of the God we represent. We bear this fruit to the extent that the grace of God fills us to overflowing. In the heat of life in the office, in the class room, in the field, or in the home, our assurance that God's grace is readily available gives us courage to think and act righteously. We will experience this assurance when we trust Christ to provide for us. Otherwise we will be anxious in the face of every challenge. Then there will be no fruit, no demonstration of the trustworthiness and glory of God. No demonstration, no significance.

> O eternal God, I want to be like Jeremiah's blessed tree. Plant me by your river of grace with full confidence that it will always be filled from your eternal spring of joy. Amen.

Promises for the Battle

Fruitful Courage

Patient Courage

+———+

Do not fret because of evildoers, be not envious toward wrongdoers. For they will wither quickly like the grass, and fade like the green herb. Trust in the Eternal, and do good; dwell in the land and cultivate faithfulness. Delight yourself in the Eternal and he will give you the desires of your heart. ... *Psalm 37:1-4*

Some of our anxiety comes from asking the question: "Where is the God of justice?" We see the wicked prosper, and wonder, "What profit is it to have kept his commands?" When it appears that holding stock in Jesus will detract from our joy, we worry. God's people have asked these questions from the beginning. And his answer has always been, "Look to the end." We must not judge by God's current dealings with anyone. He is kind to the wicked for several reasons: His kindness could lead them to repentance; on the other hand, it shows more clearly the wickedness of their sin as they worship their possessions. But they will surely lose it all in the end. Their temporal success is no guarantee of eternal joy. If we set God before us as our source of joy, if we do the good he commands, and if we wait for his perfectly timed justice, we will overcome the anxiety in our hearts.

> Gracious God, anxiety in my heart weighs it down, but your good word makes it glad again. Grant me the confidence to wait patiently for your promises in Jesus' name.

Patient Courage

Victorious Courage

†———†

These things I have spoken to you, so that in me you may have peace. In the world you have tribulation, but take courage; I have overcome the world. *John 16:33* (NASB)

Here is another reminder of what is possible for us *in Jesus*. We can be courageous because Jesus fought and won the same battles we must fight and win. He encountered ridicule for his confidence in a God he could not define or manipulate. He encountered resistance to the good news of the establishment of his kingdom. He encountered rottenness at every level of his culture. Because he trusted the Father's glorious promises, wise counsel and powerful control over the events of history, he overcame this tribulation. The world was wrong about all that is important. Because of Jesus' victory, sin is now defined in terms of faith in him. Righteousness is verified by his resurrection. And judgment is certified in the condemnation of Satan. The promise of this verse is that he will help us win these encounters, if we abide in him. By the power of his Spirit, he will enable our faith, loyalty, and righteousness, so that his victory is ours as well.

> Risen Savior, your promises to overcomers are overwhelming. As I face tribulation today let me see clearly the empty cross and the empty tomb. Let me remember our union so I can fully enjoy your peace.

Promises for the Battle

Victorious Courage

Reasonable Courage

✝ ✝

"Do not fear, for I am with you; do not anxiously look about you, for I am your God. I will strengthen you, surely I will help you, surely I will uphold you with my righteous right hand. ..." says the Eternal, even your Redeemer, the Holy One of Israel. *Isaiah 41:10 &14*

God could hardly be more emphatic about why we should be courageous. How ever dark the shadow in the valley, we should walk boldly in the footsteps of Christ. How ever the winds of change may swirl, our feet should be like the hind's feet on high places. Such courage is possible as we consider the promise of God's presence: he does not leave us alone, nor does he leave us with just anyone. He himself is with us in all of his godness: his supernatural strength will sustain us, and he will be righteous in how he accomplishes our deliverances, in that it will be done in accordance with his commitment to the maintenance and display of his glory. The certainty of the thrice repeated promise is sealed with three encouraging names: the Eternal — Fountain of Life, Redeemer — Closest Kinsman Savior, and the Holy One of Israel — Most Valuable Person.

> Lord Jesus, in the midst of the turmoil of society, cause me to remember you are with me. When I hesitate, cause me to remember I have your strength. In the dark, cause me to see the glory of your goodness and love.

Promises for the Battle

Reasonable Courage

Courageously Righteous

+———+

Since no one can successfully serve both God and mammon... do not be anxious for your life, ... nor for your body, ... for life is certainly more than food, and the body than clothing. ... Do not be anxious ... for your heavenly Father knows that you need all these things. But seek first his kingdom and his righteousness; and all these things shall be added to you. *Matthew 6:24-34*

"What we hope in we worship; what we worship we serve," a wise man once said. Jesus said we must look to God as our source of hope, so that we see him as having ultimate worth in our eyes, so we do what is necessary to obtain the benefits he offers. He promises that God will provide for our needs if we own him as king, and if we obey his rules in such a way that he is seen as a good and wise ruler. Then we will have the courage to live righteous lives. If we try to feather our own nests, we register a vote of no confidence in God and live in a constant state of anxiety, not only about having enough for today, but enough for tomorrow as well. Fortunately, our King is also a heavenly Father, who knows exactly what we need and is glad to give us the kingdom and all that he as our Father/King can provide.

> Heavenly Father, unless I had believed I would see your goodness in the land of the living, I would have despaired. Grant me strength to wait hopefully for you today.

Courageously Righteous

Encouraged Praise

If the Eternal had not been my help, my soul would soon have dwelt in silence. If I should say, "My foot has slipped," your lovingkindness, O Eternal, will hold me up. When my anxious thoughts multiply within me, your consolations delight my soul. *Psalm 94:17-19*

O Lord, how often have I felt like Jehoshaphat in face of the armies of Ammon and Moab, when he cried, We are powerless before this great multitude, nor do we know what to do, but our eyes are on you." And how often you have consoled my soul by powerfully working on my behalf. Thank you for the memory of Scripture in which I see evidence of your loving salvation in situations far worse than mine. Thank you for bringing to mind the countless times you have filled my cup to overflowing and spread a table before me in the presence of my enemies. In the seemingly most hopeless situations you gave me reason to sing: "Fresh courage take; the clouds you so much dread are big with mercy, and shall break with blessings on your head!" The surprises of your mercy overcame every anxious thought. Who is like you, O Lord? There is no Rock besides you; no Creator, Redeemer, Defender, Protector, who has proved himself repeatedly as the only sovereign source of security and stability and freedom in a changing and uncertain world. Amen.

Promises for the Battle

Encouraged Praise

Forgiveness

✦━━━✦

When we carry a bitter spirit in our hearts we are guilty of unbelief. Being bitter means we do not believe God will or can adequately dispense justice in the world. So we harbor an unforgiving spirit; we angrily and continually view our adversaries as enemies. This bitterness eventually obliterates our joy and poisons everyone near us. Our unwillingness to forgive even blocks our access to God's forgiveness, for the Lord will not forgive those who distrust his ability to exercise his right to be the judge of all the earth. But God has communicated many promises that beautifully present the joys of a forgiving heart.

A Bigger Picture

+——+

> You meant harm against me; God meant it for good in order to bring about this present result, to preserve many people alive. So therefore, do not be afraid; I will provide for you and your little ones. *Genesis 50:19-21*

Joseph's ability to see beyond the immediate cause of his misadventures years before, enabled him to be merciful and gracious to his antagonists. If we will learn to see the truth of all the hurtful events in our lives as Joseph saw his, no bitterness will ever creep in. We will be able to forgive, because we will perceive our enemies as agents of God's good, not only to us, but also to many others as well. Joseph saw that God sovereignly acted for his good through the evil intentions of his brothers. Therefore he was able to continue to trust God during his captivity, so that he did not give in to temptation. He was able to trust God during his sovereignty, so that he used it for good, not revenge. As we acknowledge the wisdom and power of God as he acts in our lives through our enemies, we will avoid the bitterness that will keep them from sharing in his grace to us.

> O wise and mighty Ruler of all creation, remove the blinders of my pride, so I can see the larger purpose behind my pain, and can forgive the agents of your good who caused it. Amen.

A Bigger Picture

Sweet Hearts

✜

Let all bitterness ... be put away from you along with all malice, and be kind to one another: tenderhearted, forgiving each other, just as God in Christ also has forgiven you. *Ephesians 4:31-32*

Total commitment to good relationships is what the Doctor orders. He orders it, and he has shown us what is involved in such a life by living it himself. We put away all bitterness so we can have the same joy in relationships the Father now enjoys with those of us who are "in Christ." This means *all* bitterness. A little leaven leavens the whole lump; a little bitterness taints the sweetness of our attitude toward someone who has hurt us, and makes tenderheartedness impossible. We can put away the pain we feel and the revenge we desire, because God promised to accomplish his justice through Christ; because we will experience the joy of not having an enemy; and because we will expand the fullness of our forgiveness by extending it to others — forgiving another's hurt clears room in our hearts to cherish God's grace to us and to see how complete it is as we extend it beyond ourselves.

> Gracious and forgiving Father, cause me to treasure the mercy you have given me. Help me let go of all the pain I have cherished from the hurts of others, so I can be full of the joy of your mercy to me in Jesus. Amen.

Sweet Hearts

Prophylactic Grace

+———+

> See to it that no one comes short of the grace of God; that no root of bitterness springing up causes trouble, and by it many be defiled. *Hebrews 12:15* (NASB)

While this is stated in the form of a command, we can see the promise in the midst of it: if we maintain a good flow of God's grace into our lives, bitterness will not sprout in our hearts, and its fruit will not pollute those who live in our sphere of influence. We shut ourselves off from *G*od's *R*escuing *A*nd *C*aring *E*xertion by ceasing to trust his disposition of events in our lives, by ceasing to trust him to right the wrongs done to us, and by ceasing to trust him to turn stumbling blocks into stepping stones. Without the hope grace provides, we cherish the hurt, become unwilling to forgive, and enlist others in our efforts to secure the justice we feel we must have. Those who encounter us become infected with our arrogance and experience our pain. But when, by faith, we open ourselves to *G*od's *R*escuing *A*nd *C*aring *E*xertion, he flushes the virus of bitterness from our systems and prevents the infection from spreading. Then the sweet life-giving spring of eternal life can flow out of us.

> Gracious Lord, help me to see the purifying strength of your grace in my life, so I will trust you to overcome the hurt I have felt and my bitterness will be banished. Amen.

Promises for the Battle

Prophylactic Grace

Heavenly Warning

My heavenly Father will make every one of you pay your debts to him if you do not forgive your brother from your heart. Matthew 18:35

The old saying goes, "You always hurt the one you love." Scripture consistently confirms this truth: "you shall not take vengeance, nor bear any grudge against the sons of your people, but you shall surely love your neighbor as yourself; I am the Eternal [who redeemed you]." It is the neighbor/family member who does us wrong, against whom we desire revenge, but for whom we must cultivate great affection. The road to this wonderful love climbs the mountain of forgiveness. To ascend it we must put the offense behind us so we can view an enemy as valuable in our eyes. Jesus' warning will help us up this mountain. Wanting to continue as a beneficiary of God's merciful grace, and not wanting to pay for our own sins, will keep us from seeking happiness in the small satisfaction our own efforts at revenge will bring us. God's forgiveness opens the door to all the joy we desire. Bitterness closes that door by saying it isn't enough.

> Father, I look at what you did for me in the cross of Christ. Please help me see clearly how little I can gain from being bitter, and how much I stand to lose by refusing to forgive with all my heart. Amen.

Heavenly Warning

Trusting Example

> Christ left you an example to follow. ... When he was reviled, he did not revile in return; when he suffered he did not threaten; but he trusted to him who judges justly. *1 Peter 2:21-23*

No one was wronged worse than Jesus. No one got a raw deal as bad as his. No one was abused more. No one was rejected more. And no one was as innocent. So what did he do when his heart filled with moral indignation? He did not lash out in self-righteous indignation. He did not call ten thousand angels. Instead, he handed over his grievance to God. Why? Because he knew that the Judge of all the earth would do right. He knew the Father, whose glory he honored, would not abandon anyone who lived this way. For God's righteousness consists in acting in a way that honors his own glory. He will vindicate those who trust him because he will always vindicate his reputation for holiness. Confident of this, Jesus never allowed any sinful bitterness to arise in his heart. And we shouldn't either. We battle bitterness by trusting our vindication to God's perfect justice. If we keep a grudge, we doubt the Judge.

> O Righteous Judge, I rest my case at the foot of the cross, where Jesus made me righteous and showed me how to fully rely on your wisdom and power to secure my joy. Amen.

Trusting Example

Fretless Forgiveness

He will bring forth your righteousness as the light, and your judgment as the noonday. Rest in the Eternal and wait patiently for him; do not fret because of him who prospers in his way, because of the man who carries out wicked schemes. Cease from anger, and forsake wrath; do not fret, it leads only to evil-doing. *Psalm 37:6-8*

Appearances can be deceiving. Someone with acute appendicitis does not appear to be in danger. Someone with all the trappings of professional and social success does not appear to be in spiritual danger either. Someone who gains an advantageous position by hurting us only appears to prosper. By not taking vengeance we only appear to lose. But we can let go of the anger associated with the pain we have experienced because: 1) God will make our righteousness clear by causing our way to prosper in the end. When we look back from the joyful fellowship of heaven, we'll know how right we were. 2) Forgiving the one who hurt us will keep us from perpetuating the evil. James tells us "the anger of man does not work the righteousness of God." In this case negative times negative would not produce a positive.

> Lord, your eyes are on the righteous and your ears are open to my cry. You will strongly support me if my heart is completely yours. O let it be. Amen.

Fretless Forgiveness

Saving Forgiveness

> Be on your guard against destroying faith! If your brother sins, rebuke him; and if he repents, forgive him. And if he sins against you seven times a day, and returns to you seven times, saying, "I repent," forgive him. *Luke 17:3-4*

We have both the responsibility and the opportunity to strengthen the faith of our brothers and sisters in Christ. One of the most obvious ways we can do this is by forgiving them. For when we forgive, we show how wonderful Jesus' forgiveness is to us. In fact, if we don't forgive other believers who sin against us, we will drive them away from their faith in Christ and will suffer the "woe" he will direct toward us. But Jesus promises us that if we stand guard over our own hearts, to keep bitterness from gaining a foothold, we will even be able to forgive repeat offenders. This forgiveness will encourage them to grow in their confidence that Jesus is able to create a community of love in which they can mature as members of God's family. And it will keep us going to him for the security, stability and freedom we need to go on cheerfully in the face of adversity.

> Gracious Lord, I enjoy being in your community of love. Help me to extend your forgiving grace to those who have hurt me, so I will avoid placing stumbling blocks in the way of their faith. Amen.

Saving Forgiveness

Pardoning Praise

+———+

You shall not hate your brother in your heart; ... you shall not take vengeance, nor bear any grudge ... but you shall love your neighbor as yourself; for I am the Eternal ... who brought you out of the land of Egypt.
Leviticus 19:19

Mercy, grace and peace are gifts from you, O God, which I cherish especially because of what you have done to make them mine. Just as you brought the Children of Israel out of bondage in Egypt with mighty works, so you have delivered me from my bondage to sin and from the threat it held against my happiness. "There is no condemnation to those who are in Christ Jesus." So I love the mercy I have received from you. Even more, I cherish the freedom that comes with my forgiveness, especially the freedom from having to insure my own vengeance and vindication. Especially when others have caused me pain, I cherish the freedom to restore the relationship because of what Jesus did at Calvary. What a joy it is to know that judgment and justice are safe in your hands! What a joy it is to be relieved of that terrible burden, so that I can be free to extend your grace even to my enemies! Thank you, O Most Merciful, for the privilege of participating in the dispensation of your forgiving love, by the power of your Spirit, in the Name of Jesus. Amen & Amen!

Promises for the Battle

Pardoning Praise

Freedom

✝———✝

One definition of freedom is having the mental, moral and material resources to do what we want to do. Not having access to these resources keeps us from living freely. Fear that we won't have access to these resources also keeps us from living freely. Certain access comes only when we entrust our futures to Jesus, because God's grace flows only to his disciples. Living by faith also enables us to use our freedom wisely. So God encourages our freedom with many promises to supply all our needs through Jesus.

Gracious Freedom

✢

It was for freedom that Christ set us free; therefore keep standing firm and do not be subject again to a yoke of slavery. ... For you were called to freedom, brethren; only do not turn your freedom into an opportunity for the flesh, but through love serve one another. *Galatians 5:1, 13* (NASB)

By virtue of a relationship with Jesus, we can be free: free from legalism, from the power of Satan, from fear of what others may do to us, and from the cultural restrictions of the mosaic law. But the freedom we have in Christ is not just freedom *from* problems, it is freedom to pursue the fullness of life. For example, a large and unexpected inheritance frees us to choose whatever lifestyle we desire. Similarly, a patient, whose doctor releases him from the confinement of his disease, is free to live as healthy people live. So being delivered from the poverty of self-sufficiency — by faith in the future grace promised and guaranteed in Jesus — frees us to pursue the abundant life he makes available. He set us free so we can enjoy experiencing the fullness of the grace of God. This enjoyment can best be accomplished by avoiding self-indulgence, and by extending God's grace to others in love. For this shows off the satisfying completeness of our freedom as joint heirs with Christ.

> Gracious Redeemer, I still fight the inclination to grasp and to hoard, to worry and to hide. Help me to remember the freedom of your love so I can love as freely as you. Amen.

Promises for the Battle

Gracious Freedom

Related Freedom

> If you abide in my word, then you are truly disciples of mine and you shall know the truth, and the truth shall make you free. ... Truly, I say to you, whoever commits sin is the slave of sin. The slave does not remain in the house forever; but the son does remain forever. If therefore the Son makes you free, you shall be free indeed. *John 8:31-36*

Patients are not free to make wise decisions regarding health and medical care unless they know the truth about their condition and about the options available to them. They can receive this truth in their relationship with the doctor. As long as they act in accord with his instructions, they will avoid being enslaved to a disease. So we say the truth makes them free and the doctor makes them free. And both propositions are true. Since the world in which we live is filled with children of the Devil, who doesn't want us to know what's going on, we must stay close to Jesus. For only he accurately conveys the Father's design for living. The truth we see in, and hear from, Jesus about the Father's goodness, wisdom, and power shows us how much better we will be if we live righteously. Joyful sin-free living depends on truth-full living.

> Holy Father, I want to be a true disciple of your Son by living according to his word. But I hear so much noise around me. Cause the joy of his freedom to make me hear his voice more clearly above the crowd. Amen.

Related Freedom

Morally Free

+———+

Forgiveness of sins is proclaimed to you through Jesus, and through him everyone who believes is freed from all the things, from which you could not be freed through the Law of Moses. *Acts 13:38-39*

Forgiveness and freedom, that's good news! That's the Gospel! As good as the Law was, it could not free us from the inclination to change God's commands from a doctor's prescription for which we must praise, into a job description for which we demand praise. The Law taught us to live by faith, but it could not change our legalistic hearts. Now, however, in Christ, the Holy Spirit has given us new hearts, hearts inclined to welcome God's Word, so "the requirement of the Law might be fulfilled in us." The name for this kind of freedom is *moral freedom*. Before the regenerating work of the Spirit, we were physically able to trust God, but morally unable, because we didn't *want* to trust him. So we were not free to love our enemies because we didn't *want* to love them. Now, in Christ, we are free from our bondage to hatred and all the trouble that goes with it, because we *want* to trust God's promise that he will provide more for us than our enemies can ever take away.

> Lord Jesus, you have changed me by the transforming power of a new affection. Keep me trusting your promises so I will remain free of the legalistic tendencies of my flesh. Amen.

Morally Free

Freedom From Fear

What then shall we say to these truths of God's sovereign work? We say, if God is for us, who is against us? He who did not spare his own Son, but delivered him up for us all, how will he not also with him freely give us all things? *Romans 8:31-32*

Freedom from fear rests in the grace of God. It rests on knowing how fully and effectively and joyously he has worked for us in the past, especially through Jesus. It rests on knowing, by implication, that such grace will continue to be with us, no matter what kind of obstacles to our joy we encounter. The God who can satisfy his desire to do good to ungodly people, while righteously upholding the glory of his goodness, can be trusted to overcome every obstacle that might arise to impede the flow of his blessing. Furthermore, God's grace is freeing because he is free. He is free in that the joy he experiences as he beholds his perfection in the Son is all that compels him to do everything necessary to bring his people into this same experience. Therefore we are released from fearing anything that appears to get in the way of his accomplishing this purpose. If the God of grace is for us, no one can effectively be against us.

> Gracious God, keep me from judging you by feeble sense. I want to trust you for your grace. I know that behind your frowning providence, you hide a smiling face. Amen.

Freedom From Fear

Reliable Freedom

✧───✧

Let your character be free from the love of money,
being content with what you have; for God has said,
"I will never desert you, nor will I ever forsake you,"
Hebrews 13:5

God tells us in this promise that he is both sufficient for us and satisfying to us. If he weren't, what difference would it make if he stayed with us? He would merely be an albatross around our necks. His presence would compel us to love money so much that we would arrange our lives in order to gain as much benefit as money can provide. But God is infinitely more beneficial and more trustworthy than money. To prove this he sent Jesus to reconcile us to himself; and because of Jesus' atoning death, we have the Holy Spirit living in us, pouring the love the members of the Trinity have for one another into our hearts. Our God is a god who works for those who wait for him. In contrast, when money is our god, we must work to secure its benefits for us. So if we will continually compare the stability, security, and satisfying activity of our committed God with the passivity, vulnerability, and volatility of money, our hearts will be free from the love of money, completely satisfied with God and his gifts.

> Reliable Lord, open my eyes to see how faithful you are and how involved you are in my daily life. And help me to see how anxious and weary are those who find their delight in what money can do for them. Keep me from idolatry. Amen.

Reliable Freedom

Glorious Freedom

Whenever someone turns to the Lord, the veil is taken away. The Lord is the Spirit; and where the Spirit of the Lord is, there is freedom. And we each, with unveiled face reflecting the glory of the Lord, are being transformed into the same image from glory to glory. *2 Corinthians 3:17-18*

"Aha!" experiences are not only wonderful all by themselves, they are also wonderful because they are so freeing. Vast new possibilities open before us when the light finally goes on. We see relationships we did not know existed. We foresee connections and projects that otherwise never could have developed. This is the kind of freedom Paul has in mind in these verses. Becoming a Christian is the best of these "Aha!" experiences. The Holy Spirit freed us by enabling us to perceive and appreciate "the glory of God in the face of Christ" when we heard the Gospel. Now as we continue to view all God has shown us of himself in Scripture, we see the panorama of life as God intends us to live it, rather than the narrow restricted view of our sinful self-centeredness. As our exposure to the glory of God increases, we absorb more of that glory, and our capacity to extend it to others grows as well. With this kind of freedom all our circumstances become stepping stones to more courage and joy.

> Glorious Lord, grant me wisdom as I seek to use my freedom to bring others into the same experience of your glory that I enjoy. Amen.

Glorious Freedom

Submissive Freedom

+———+

What then is my reward? That, when I preach the gospel, I may offer the gospel without charge, so as not to make full use of my right in the gospel. For though I am free from all, I have made myself a slave to all, that I might win the more. *1 Corinthians 9:18-19* (NASB)

Cultural restraints do not bind Christians. We are free to eat what we want, drink what we want, wear what we want, and socialize with whom we want. When Jesus freed us from the dietary and cultic practices of the Mosaic Law, he freed us from every other tradition of every other culture at the same time. Along with this freedom comes another, equally encompassing freedom, the freedom to submit for the sake of the Gospel. Because cultural distinctives don't make any difference in our relationship with Christ, we can assume many different cultural postures, so long as they do not involve living contrary to the teaching of God. In fact Paul indicates that since we have the first freedom, we should use the second. We have been made free from culture, *in order that* we accommodate to many cultures — including our culture, *in order that* we penetrate these cultures — including our culture — with the liberating truth of Jesus Christ. The joy of this freedom makes it most rewarding.

> With this promise, O Lord, I need understanding so I can discern what is culturally significant and what is culturally dangerous, and wisdom so I can choose well for Jesus' sake. Amen.

Submissive Freedom

Freedom that Praises

✟————✟

Thanks be to God that though you were slaves of sin, you became obedient from the heart to that form of teaching to which you were committed, and having been freed from sin, you became slaves of righteousness.
Romans 6:17-18 (NASB)

Liberating Lord, I have never felt so free as in being bound to you. When I was enslaved to my commitment to self-sufficiency and self-exaltation, I had only a terrible prospect of suffering your wrath. For the wages of sin is death. I didn't even know it; so I was bound by ignorance as well as iniquity. Now, having been freed from my sin, I can enjoy the freedom of being enslaved to you. Commitment to entrust my future to you frees me from the fear of bearing that burden on my own. Seeing your rules for life as the best way to live frees me to experience the joy of your approval and blessing. Following you in the obedience of faith frees me to be of benefit to people everywhere. What's more amazing is that being enslaved to you, as I live righteously before you, gives me access to your presence. Because of my commitment to you, you are committed to allow me to enter with the saints and angels for worship, adoration and praise. How blessed am I, O God who made heaven and earth, who keeps faith forever, and who sets the prisoner free with the gift of eternal life! Amen.

Freedom that Praises

Thinking

To succeed as a Christian in this fast paced world, we must make the time and effort to think about God and about how well we are living in accord with his design. Haphazard, lazy thought processes are dangerous; they indicate we are not trusting God. To be people of faith, we must be thinking people. For God rewards those who think his thoughts after him. He blesses us when we consider and ponder and contemplate him, his works, and the ideas he has communicated to us. He never demands we trust him blindly; he always expects our faith to be reasoned because he's so reasonable.

Transforming Thoughts

✝——✝

Whatever is true, whatever is honorable, whatever is right, whatever is pure, whatever is lovely, whatever is of good repute, if there is any excellence and if anything worthy of praise, let your mind dwell on these things. Philippians 4:8

Transformation comes from renewing the mind as well as the heart. God gives us a new heart by the work of the Spirit. We give ourselves a new mind by changing its content. Unfortunately we can't dump out all of the evil material we have accumulated over the years. But we can crowd it away from the central pathways on which our thoughts run by moving in new material. The more we entertain, consider, and review information God deems compatible with the glory of his goodness, the less we will recall and dwell on what offends him. Like wagons following ruts in a muddy road, our thoughts will travel more readily down our mind's most used paths. Besides the joy experienced in constant encounters with good, and besides the difference such thinking will make in our relationships with other people, we realize the hope of fellowship with God. Contemplating real good brings peace and wholeness to our souls. What better environment can we create for the "God of Peace" when he comes to walk with us in the garden?

> O Lord, teach me to love what you love, to enjoy what you enjoy, so I can think your thoughts after you, so when we talk, we experience the most wonderful fellowship. Amen.

Transforming Thoughts

Sanctifying Consideration

Consider yourselves to be dead to sin, but alive to God in Christ Jesus. Therefore do not let sin reign in your mortal body for the purpose of obeying its lusts.
Romans 6:11-12

Jesus is dead to sin — it has no authority to condemn him or control his behavior — and we are united with Jesus. He lives to God — the fellowship of the Father and Son is unbroken by any dissension between them — and we are linked to Jesus. So union with Christ is the foundation of our hope that we can overcome the sin which still dwells in us. Because we were included in his crucifixion, we shall be included in his resurrection. These truths make a difference as we interact with them. We activate their power by meditating on them until the richness and beauty of being linked to Jesus overwhelms us. In the age to come, the surpassing riches of the glory of God will be extended only to those who are in Christ. Union with Christ promises a future in which we can be certain it is possible to overcome sin. Believing this promise removes the despair we would otherwise feel as we encounter strong desires for things which dishonor God. Through Jesus we have access to the grace of God, particularly to a change of heart that allows us to delight in the work of God. So if we think carefully about our fellowship with God through our union with Jesus, righteousness will reign in our lives, not sin.

> Lord, open my eyes to all the benefits of being one with you, so I can see them clearly, love them dearly, and follow you more truly. Amen.

Sanctifying Consideration

Considering History

+———+

> By faith Abraham, when he was tested, offered up Isaac ... his only begotten son; to whom it was said, "In Isaac your descendants shall be called." He considered that God is able to raise men even from the dead.
> *Hebrews 11:17-19*

When Abraham went down to Egypt to escape the famine, and sold his wife into the harem to escape the Pharaoh; he was dead to the promises of God. For he could not have a child who would bless the nations, nor inherit the land, if his wife was not his. But the Eternal rescued him from an impossible situation. When Abraham was ninety nine years old the Eternal gave him a firm date for the birth of the son he had promised. By then both Abraham and Sarah were too old to conceive a child on their own, and they knew it. While they contemplated their bodies, both as good as dead, they did not waver in unbelief, but acted in accordance with the promise, receiving Isaac in due time. So faith comes not just by hearing the promises of God, but also by considering our experiences with the God who promises. Abraham had already seen God "raise him from the dead" twice. As he walked up the mountain with Isaac, he considered all this, and concluded he was able and willing to do it again.

> Glorious God, help me to think of your graciousness and faithfulness in my life, so when you put me in tight places, I walk forward in faith, eager to see you raise me up too. Amen.

Considering History

Captivating Thoughts

> We do not war according to the flesh. ... We are destroying speculations and every lofty thing raised up against the knowledge of God, and we are taking every thought captive to make it obey Christ. *2 Corinthians 10:3-5*

Satan's primary strategy for defeating our faith is to build walls of lies, half-truths, and innuendo. Slowly he connects each untruthful brick until they become fortresses of falsehood by which he controls larger and larger sections of our cognitive landscape. He suggests God's inability and unwillingness to be a secure and stable source of joy. He encourages futile speculations about our own ability to provide a satisfying future. He promotes programs that appeal to our desire to be self-sufficient and self-congratulatory. But if we fight the fight of faith in our minds, we will succeed in remaining confident and in living righteously. For as we think in our hearts, so we live. If we make the words of God sentinels that stand guard at our eyes and ears, every idea seeking entrance can be challenged, every suggestion monitored, every impression examined. We can even enlist these soldiers to pull the bricks out of Satan's walls and restructure them under Jesus' directions into bulwarks against further attacks.

> Gracious Master, strengthen the arms of my heart as I raise the "Sword of the Spirit" to battle the strongholds in my soul. Guide my aim and give me courage, for Jesus' sake.

Captivating Thoughts

Invigorating Thinking

✜

Consider him who has endured such hostility by sinners against himself, so that you who are losing heart may not grow weary. *Hebrews 12:2-3*

Because we all want to belong and to be loved, hostility is particularly trying. We see the animosity of family and colleagues as life-threatening. How can we live if those we see every day do not have our best interests in mind? So we think about forsaking the fellowship of God and the promise of eternal joy for the momentary pleasures of comfort and human companionship. We are not alone. Jesus struggled with this too. When almost everyone around him contradicted the truth he spoke, how did he keep from becoming weary enough to quit? He remembered his Father was using this antipathy to strengthen his desire for the goodness of Heaven. He did not regard lightly the discipline of the Lord. Rather he saw it as necessary to produce in him the strongest possible delight in what God set before him. Thinking about the Father's presence and purpose in the midst of his pain kept him from giving up. He also remembered that God judges justly and rewards those who remain true to their covenant with him. He endured infinitely more rejection than we will; so imitating Jesus' mental and spiritual processes will produce similar results in us as well.

> Perfect Father, when I seem overwhelmed help me to remember your faithfulness to Jesus so I can follow him in the obedience of faith.

Invigorating Thinking

Maturing Consideration

Consider it all joy, my brethren, when you encounter various trials, because the testing of your faith produces endurance. Let endurance have its perfect result, so you may be perfect and complete, lacking in nothing.
James 1:2-4

In the best sense of the word James is a pragmatist. He is concerned that we survive long enough in the faith to mature. And he knows we will not survive if we don't teach ourselves to look at our everyday circumstances from the right perspective. We must remove ourselves from the immediate distress of difficulties by using our mind as an observation platform. From this vantage point we can see the good result possible, because we see more than just the difficulty. As a woman in labor looks beyond the suffering of the delivery to the birth of her child, so we must look beyond every trial to the character development God desires us to attain, and to the benefits of that maturity. If we take the time to consider, to ponder, to weigh, and to appraise the result of continuing to trust in God, we will be more likely to ward off Satan's fiery darts. Consideration helps us see the joy of fellowship that will be ours, and feeds on that joy, so we will have strength to endure until the Lord fulfills his promises.

> Thank you Father for providing enough resistance to my faith that it might grow stronger as I press forward to the eternal joy promised in your Word. Amen.

Maturing Consideration

Insightful Consideration

Consider what I say, for the Lord will give you understanding in everything. *2 Timothy 2:7*

God's hope for Bible readers: If we exert ourselves to think carefully about what he has said, he will bless us with insight; we will be able to view reality the same way God's prophet saw it. God is not a god of confusion. He does not speak to us in order to keep us in the dark. He wants us to walk in the light as he is in the light. So we can assume that his communication is understandable. Yet we cannot presume we will be able to achieve understanding without effort. God doesn't short circuit the means he has established to achieve the ends he desires. If we learn the ins and outs of grammar and syntax, God will honor our efforts. If we master the nuances of our vocabulary, God will reward our endeavors. If we discipline ourselves to spend time pondering what he says, our investment will pay great dividends. If we come humbly — willing to see things from God's perspective — to have our ideas changed, and to be transformed by the truth we encounter, he promises we will go away with new minds, satisfied hearts, and growing discernment.

> Eternal Word, speak to my heart as I engage your written word. Keep me from twisting it to suit my view of reality. And grant me an appreciation for your wonderful truth. Amen.

Insightful Consideration

Considered Praise

✦━━✦

One generation shall praise your works to another, declaring your mighty acts. On the glorious splendor of your majesty, and on your wonderful works, I will meditate. Many shall speak of the power of your awesome acts, and I will tell of your greatness.
Psalm 145:4-6

Glorious God, elegant design and exquisite detail characterize the creation you spoke into being and sustain by the power of your word. For thousands of years flora and fauna have flourished according to the instructions you devised and introduced into each interconnected species. Throughout human history you intervened so we might continue to experience your goodness, keeping us from destroying ourselves in the process. You did not leave us without a witness. Regardless of how evil we became, you retained a remnant who followed you in the obedience of faith. Even more, you opened our eyes to discover the rules that govern creation, so we can manage it wisely and beneficially. But best and most amazing of all, you sent your Son to deliver me from the penalty and power of the sin which kept me from enjoying the glory of your work. By wisely using your power, the infinite God took on human form and received my punishment. You raised him from the dead, and, because of your love for him, drew millions to worship you in his name. In this brilliant light, I discern and delight in the glorious splendor of all your other deeds. Hallelujah!

Considered Praise

Patience

When we are impatient we have a strong sense that we should be getting on with some course of action or project, and that we are not well-advised simply to let God work for us and through us as we wait for him. Our desire to be great causes us to stop waiting on God to work in and through us according to his good pleasure. So impatience is turning away in unbelief from God to find satisfaction in our own uninterrupted plan of action. Since faith, at root, is a sense of satisfaction with a promise of perfectly timed future grace, God has given us promises perfectly designed to promote patience.

Wisely Patient

The end of a matter is better than its beginning. Patience of spirit is better than haughtiness of spirit. Do not be eager in your heart to be angry, for anger resides in the bosom of fools. *Ecclesiastes 7:8-9* (NASB)

God is perfectly wise. From him we learn that wisdom consists in the ability to discern and choose what will give us the greatest joy over the longest period of time. Only a fool would make a choice that would be harmful in the end, however pleasant it might seem in the beginning. So wise people are patient people, especially when we are confronted with painful situations in which we might become angry. Since we don't know with certainty how a series of events will conclude, we act wisely if we wait patiently for God to finish what he began. The arrogant pride that leads to easy anger will not bring us any lasting joy; for "the anger of man does not accomplish the righteousness of God." Rather it only drives people away from us and away from God. On the other hand a patient spirit allows God time to turn stumbling blocks into stepping stones that bring us and our adversaries closer to each other and to him, our perfect source of joy.

> Sovereign Lord, you know the end from the beginning, and you desire nothing but my good. So I reaffirm my trust in your wise disposition of my circumstances. Grant me the grace of a humble, patient spirit in my most painful situations. Amen.

Wisely Patient

"Post-its" For Patience

✢————✢

Record the vision and inscribe it on tablets, that the one who reads it may run. For the vision is yet for the appointed time; it hastens toward the goal, and it will not fail. Though it tarries, wait for it; for it will certainly come, it will not delay. Habakkuk 2:2-3 (NASB)

Sometimes the Lord assures us of his solution to our problems long before he actually accomplishes it. When we go back to him wondering why he has not brought us relief yet, he patiently explains that his timing is perfect; so we would be wise to keep following his direction in our lives, while we wait for him to fulfill his promises. Habakkuk learned this while he waited for the Lord to deliver Israel from the Assyrians. Later we read that "at the right time Christ died for the ungodly." What an encouragement! The Lord responds to our impatience with a patient reminder that he has the situation well in hand. He exhibits his understanding of our emotional frailty by telling us to keep the promises where we can see them; for he knows that we need frequent reminding if our faith is to remain strong. God's word to Habakkuk is a promise that will keep us trusting God's promises.

> Father, how glad I am that you know me so well. Thank you for showing me how to keep trusting and keep going as I wait patiently for you to bring about the good you have promised and guaranteed through Jesus. Amen.

"Post-its" For Patience

Longsuffering Love

Love produces a willingness to suffer at length. 1 Corinthians 13:4

What good news! If we are having difficulty being patient with irritating individuals, love will enable us to suffer that irritation at some length while we continue to work for their good. Love exists in us as we see another person as valuable to us. When we adjust our sight picture we can be patient with the person who cuts us off in traffic, with the person who constantly makes excuses for poor choices, and with the one who takes advantage of us at every turn. The patience of love is different than just gritting our teeth in angry endurance. The longsuffering of love appears as a gracious and sweet spirit that waits until our adversary is ready to receive the good we have to offer. This expression of love for others flows in large part from the joy we have in God as he satisfies our need to be loved. When we are thoroughly delighted with him, we seek the greater joy of bringing others into our happiness. Rather than give up such joy, we become willing to suffer at some length so that we can help someone else experience the Lord's grace that made us so happy.

> Loving Lord, you have caused me to drink from the "river of your delights." Thank you for such fulfilling affection. May I so enjoy your love that I am willing to wait to share it with my enemy in Jesus' name. Amen.

Promises for the Battle

Longsuffering Love

Hopeful Patience

✝———✝

Be longsuffering; strengthen your hearts, for the coming of the Lord is at hand. Do not complain, brethren, against one another, that you yourselves may not be judged. ... Those who spoke in the Lord's name are an example of patience and longsuffering. Behold, we count those fortunate who endured. *James 5:8-11*

If we had no hope, no certainty, that the Lord would provide an eternal future of happy tomorrows, it would be very difficult to endure, especially the antagonism and annoyances of colleagues and friends. It would be very difficult to stand for what is right when those around us are falling for what is wrong. But the Lord certainly will return to "vindicate his chosen ones" who maintain the faith in the face of difficulties. Moses didn't complain when Israel rebelled in the wilderness. He prayed for God not to give up on them; for he trusted in God's commitment to glorify himself by doing the impossible. When Israel demanded a human king, Samuel remained so committed to them that he continued to pray diligently for them; for he trusted in God's willingness to forgive and renew sinful people. So we count them both among the fortunate whom God has satisfied. And we can count ourselves fortunate to have such hopefully patient examples.

> O God, I see how you have blessed those who trust you enough to continue patiently to do right in the face of opposition. Grant me to know the joy they knew as I await the return of Jesus. Amen.

Hopeful Patience

Power for Patience

> We pray for you and ask that you may be filled with the knowledge of God's will in all spiritual wisdom and understanding, so that you may walk in a manner worthy of the Lord ... strengthened with all power, according to his glorious might, unto all steadfastness and longsuffering patience. *Colossians 1:9-11*

When we are at war the commander devises and initiates a plan for conquering an objective. When the officers and the NCOs understand the commander's intent and patiently act in accordance with this plan, they show how valuable the plan is, bringing glory to the commander. Patience demonstrates our knowledge and faith in the plan and the excellence of the planner. So patient living is worthy of the Lord, for it reflects how wise and powerful God really is as he leads us through life. Patient living comes from knowing and understanding Jesus' plan for his people, and from agreeing that it is a good one. Patient longsuffering is not from our innate ability but from our appreciation of the value of God's plan. Because he wants us to be more patient, God answers our prayers for insight and wisdom. As knowledge comes in the correct dosage and frequency, we see the excellent end he has in view and gain the power to live patiently in the present.

> Lord, thank you for making patience possible. Thank you for letting me know what you are doing, and for allowing me to be part of it with you. Make me strong in my confidence that you know what is best.

Power for Patience

Patient for Good

✛———✛

"The Eternal is my portion," says my soul, "Therefore I have hope in him. The Eternal is good to those who wait for him, to the person who seeks him." *Lamentations 3:24-25*

This promise is an excellent weapon to use in the battle against impatience, because it shows us how closely the happiness we desire is tied to our relationship with God. When we say that God is our "portion," we mean that we view him as the only one who can ultimately satisfy our hearts. He is the source of life on whom we particularly depend. The psalmist says, "God is the strength of my heart and my portion forever. For, behold, those who are far from you will perish. ... But as for me, the nearness of God is my good." Since he is utterly critical to our joy, we can wait for him to work on our behalf. We can seek time with the Lord to let him know our needs, because he delights in doing good to us when we do. Even if it takes longer than we expect for him to do us good, we can wait for him to do his absolute best. By faith we deny our urges to take matters into our own hands; for no one else can make us so certain of joy.

> Bountiful God, thank you for the presence of your Spirit who lets me know that you are my portion. I can hardly wait for you to work. In Jesus' name I come to you and patiently seek my joy in you. Amen.

Promises for the Battle

Patient for Good

Merciful Patience

✝

Christ Jesus came into the world to save sinners, among whom I am foremost; but precisely because of this I received mercy, in order that in me as the foremost, he might demonstrate his perfect longsuffering, as an example for those who were destined to put their trust in him for eternal life. *1 Timothy 1:15-16*

Before he was an apostle, Paul thought God should praise him for knowing better than he how to run his own creation. Even when he was trying to destroy the early Church, God was patient. Besides what it did for Paul, Jesus' patience with him was meant to be an encouragement for us to trust him. We should be encouraged to know that even the worst person can be redeemed. God's patience continues today. Peter tells us that this is so all of his people might repent from their arrogance. We should regard the patience of the Lord as deliverance. And Jesus' patience is an encouragement to us to be longsuffering ourselves. Patience with someone who irritates us, or patience when a situation is progressing slowly, might bring some sinner to the realization of Jesus' ability and willingness to change the most arrogant and destructive of us. Wouldn't it be excellent to have Jesus exert his patience and extend his grace and mercy through us?

> Merciful Lord, thank you for your patience with me. Thank you for the mercy I have experienced. May I so love your deliverance that I exhibit your longsuffering patience so someone else might receive your mercy too. Amen.

Promises for the Battle

Merciful Patience

The Praise of Patience

He will bring forth your righteousness as the light, and your judgment as the noonday. Therefore rest in the Eternal and wait patiently for him. *Psalm 37:6*

O wise and gracious God, every moment of my life comes from you. You have woven the tapestry of my days with infinite care and skill. The colors of my life are not a wash of random hues, but a precise pattern of contrasting and complementary living threads. Sometimes it seems that some of the colors will ruin the final product. So I look at some of the other beautiful lives you have woven and my willingness to wait returns. My patience is my praise of you. I want you to know that I trust you to do good to me with all your heart and soul. I want you to know that I trust you to cause all things to work together for good. I want you to know that I trust you to turn stumbling blocks into stepping stones. So I rest in you and try to respond to problems by extending the grace you have given me to my antagonists. I rest in you and try to wait for you to fulfill your promises. Jesus was patient with me. You keep allowing me time to repent, to experience more of your mercy. As I learn to trust you more and more, may the Spirit bring about longsuffering and patience in me. Amen.

Promises for the Battle

The Praise of Patience

Help

"Help! You know I need somebody.
"Help! Not just anybody.
"Help! You know I need someone to
"Helllpp!"

The old Beatles song couldn't have been more correct. We need help. Actually we need supernatural help. God promises much help to those who will call on him because of his reputation as a helper. Only proud unbelief would ignore such evidence. But he has even provided help to overcome our unbelief.

Holy Help

+————+

Moses said, "Do not fear! Stand by and see the salvation of the Eternal which he will accomplish for you today; for the Egyptians whom you have seen today, you will never see them again forever. The Eternal will fight for you while you keep silent." *Exodus 14:13-14*

Sometimes when we are following God, he leads us into impossible situations. God didn't part the Red Sea because Israel got lost and it was easier to part the water than to turn that mob around and head them in the right direction. They were stuck because they followed the fiery pillar and obeyed God's command through Moses. They were stuck because God had not finished teaching them about how thorough he was in his salvation. They were stuck because they needed another dose of God's glorious power before they headed to Sinai to become a nation. They were stuck because they needed to learn to replace their peevish profanity with patient prayer. It's all about worship. When Israel left Egypt, they left to worship the holy one of Israel. But they did not know him well enough to worship appropriately. So God, in his grace, put them in a desperate situation so they could learn how worthy he is to be worshiped. They needed to passionately appreciate his supremacy in all things. Helping the helpless is how he produces it.

> Who is like you among the gods, Lord Jesus? Who is like you, majestic in holiness, awesome in praises? Open my eyes to the display of your glory through my helplessness. Amen.

Holy Help

Brotherly Help

Saul went out to seek David's life while David was in the wilderness. But Jonathan arose and went to David and encouraged him in God: "Do not be afraid, for the hand of Saul my father shall not find you. Indeed, you will be king over Israel and I will be next to you." *1 Samuel 23:15–17*

God not only delivers his people from desperate situations, he also delivers them from despair. We need to overcome despair, so we don't give up while God is working out our rescue. One way he does this is by using the fellowship of another believer. Note that while Saul was looking, Jonathan knew right where to find David. More importantly, Jonathan came and "strengthened his hand in God." He didn't just tell him not to worry. He reminded David of God's promise to make him king in place of Saul. David saw God's love in Jonathan's risky effort to keep his faith alive. And David remembered God's reputation was at stake here, not his own; so God became the source of encouragement. God's renewed promise to David was like the reminder Habakkuk received that the vision was yet for the appointed time; so he should wait, for it would not be late. Renewed in his faith, David waited for the Lord to act; and God miraculously diverted Saul at the place now known as "The Rock of Escape."

Thank you, Father, for the hope of help, especially when I am ready to give up. Open my heart to the reminders of your faithfulness brought by faithful friends. Amen.

Promises for the Battle

Brotherly Help

Real Help

✝———✝

Then the Spirit of the Eternal moved Jehaziel to say, "Listen, all Judah and the inhabitants of Jerusalem and King Jehoshaphat: thus says the Eternal to you, 'Do not fear or be dismayed because of this great multitude, for the battle is not yours but God's.'" *2 Chronicles 20:14–15*

Our God is more than equal to any task we face. No matter what the odds, he is able and willing to overcome the discrepancies between us and our adversaries. When Judah was assaulted by Ethiopia, Asa prayed: "There is no one besides you to help in the battle between the powerful and those who have no strength; so help us, O Eternal, our God, for we trust in you, and in your name have come against this multitude. O Eternal, you are our God; let not man prevail against you." God answered with a mighty victory. Before God spoke similar words of comfort and deliverance to Jehoshaphat and his people, the king led the people in prayer: "We are powerless before this great multitude who are coming against us; nor do we know what to do, but our eyes are on you." So we can have hope too. For the "the eyes of the Eternal move to and fro throughout the earth that he may strongly support those whose heart is completely his." No situation is hopeless when we trust in such a God.

> O Lord, open my eyes to the reality of my need and grant me the humility to cry out to you with an honest and expectant heart. Amen.

Real Help

Hope-giving Help

+———+

> We were so afflicted in Asia, that we were burdened excessively, beyond our strength, so that we despaired even of life; indeed, we had the sentence of death within ourselves in order that we should not trust in ourselves, but in God who raises the dead. ... He on whom we have set our hope will deliver us. *2 Corinthians 1:8-10*

We won't go to be with Jesus until the time is right. When our time on earth is through, he will come to take us home, fulfilling his promise that "those who believe in me shall not see death." In the meanwhile, we may often be close to dying, or we may be in such desperate straits that we hold no hope for finding our way out. But, since our God raises the dead, we can be certain he will deliver us from every situation. If Jesus died at the right time to rescue us from the wrath of God, certainly God knows how to rescue us from less dire circumstances as well. According to Paul, the Lord uses these less drastic, but more imminently distressing situations as part of the way he delivers us from sin. For when we are clearly unable to extricate ourselves from physical danger, we more consciously entrust our lives to him immediately and for eternity. God means the experience of deliverance, to persuade us to trust him whenever temptation comes.

> Eternal God, as I rest in your power to rescue me from death forever, keep me trusting in you for deliverance from all the dangers I encounter along the way to glory. Amen.

Hope-giving Help

Teaching Help

Abraham said, "God will provide the lamb for the burnt offering." ... Then Abraham saw behind him a ram caught in the thicket. Abraham took the ram, and offered him up in the place of his son. And Abraham called the name of that place "the Eternal Will Provide."
Genesis 22:8, 13-14

Abraham was not always this confident in God. Early in their relationship, he didn't understand how absolutely trustworthy God is. So when famine came, he left the place God promised for a seemingly better place. Then, to save his skin, he forsook the woman by whom his promised son was to come, letting the king take his wife into his harem. But out of this hopelessly helpless situation God rescued him. The Lord overcame every obstacle to the receipt of his promises, even Abraham's sin. Rather than just tell Abraham to leave Egypt after God's intervention, Pharaoh gave him a military escort. Rather than antagonize Abraham, Pharaoh loaded him down with gifts. So he hastened back to Canaan and worshiped. Abraham was so sure of God's provision that he subsequently let Lot choose where he wanted to live, and he refused to receive a reward from Sodom's king. He learned what we must learn, that God will provide what he promises, especially when circumstances look bleakest.

> Almighty God, seeing how you worked with Abraham gives me hope. Work in me so that I will and do what pleases you, no matter how difficult or unreasonable it seems. Amen.

Teaching Help

Glorious Help

✠——✠

Is it not indeed from the Lord of the Universe that peoples toil for fire, and nations grow weary for nothing? For the earth will be filled with the knowledge of the glory of the Eternal as the waters cover the sea.
Habakkuk 2:13-14

God's commitment to maintain and display his glory drives his providential supervision of all of his creation. No matter how desperate our situation becomes, we can be certain God will not let the wicked succeed. He acts for his own sake, for he will not allow anyone else to accept the glory due his name. Even when he acts to rescue us, it is for the glory of his reputation. He will always work for us in a way that magnifies his reputation for holiness. Sometimes though, as in Habakkuk's case, God's mode of deliverance seems worse than the situation we are currently experiencing: God uses the ungodly to destroy the ungodly. But their wicked plans will fail as well. The fire they build from the logs of our homes will become their funeral pyre. God allows them to expend all their energy, but to gain nothing of any lasting satisfaction or significance. Therefore we can exult in the God of our salvation, who delivers us from our enemies and from our enslavement to our own success as well.

> All glory, laud, and honor belong to you, O God! In the valley of death and on the mountains of adversity you are my strength and song. Keep me trusting as you wisely unfold your plans.

Glorious Help

Unusual Help

+―――+

Jesus said to his disciples, "I have food to eat that you do not know about. ... My food is to do the will of him who sent me, and to accomplish his work." *John 4:32-34*

At the end of a long day, when we are bone-weary, frustrated, discouraged, and beat, God's deliverance often comes in the form of more work. But it's not just any work. It's not just more scutwork, not just more busy-work, not just more activity. The work which revives, rejuvenates, and restores us is work that fills the deepest reservoirs of our souls. It is work that accords with our desire to know Christ and to make him known. It is work that fans the flame of worship. It is work that doubles our joy because we are extending our joy to another. Jesus was beat when he sat down by Jacob's well. While the disciples were away trying to find bread in the middle of the day, the Father spread a banquet of ministry before his son. By bringing the woman who needed and was ready to accept his message, God rescued Jesus and kept him from falling into the morass of self-pity. He will do this for us as well. But like Jesus, we must be ready for God's food. We must train the taste buds of our hearts to long for the nourishment ministry provides.

> Lord Jesus, I want the hunger for God's will that moved you to welcome ministry as the means to lift the fatigue off your shoulders and restore the strength of your joy. Amen.

Unusual Help

Praise for the Helper

"Ah Eternal Lord! Behold, you made the heavens and the earth by your great power and by your outstretched arm! Nothing is too difficult for you." ... "Behold, I am the Eternal, the God of all flesh; is anything too difficult for me?" *Jeremiah 32:17, 27*

"Here I raise my 'Ebenezer,' hither by Thy help I've come." From Egypt to Calvary, from Mizpah to Ephesus you have delivered your people from danger and death, from difficulty and disaster. No obstacle was too great for your might. No foe was too creative or resourceful for your wisdom. Neither army nor angel, neither enemy nor environment has succeeded against your people, because you intervened, because you stepped in to rescue them. For hundreds of years you strengthened faith, purified hearts, encouraged risk, and built integrity by your marvelous and glorious rescues. Today, as I remember all you have done, I am convinced of your great love. I am convinced of your mercy and grace and your eagerness to help those who cry to you, who obey your command to call on you in the day of trouble, so that you will rescue them, and they will honor you. Because of your ability to help the hopeless and to judge the wicked, I will not fear what the godless fear. You shall be my fear, and you shall be my dread; so I shall take refuge in you through the cross, and find sanctuary in Jesus' gracious, hopeful fellowship. Amen.

Praise for the Helper

Speech

No matter how coordinated we are, one body part that is very difficult to control is our tongue. Faith plays a crucial role in what we say, and in how we say what we say. For our speech doesn't begin in the back of our throats, nor even in the back of our minds. Speech begins in our hearts. Our speech will indicate if our hearts are satisfied with all that God will do for us through Jesus, or if they're not. If our hearts are satisfied, then we will demonstrate this confidence by not using our mouths to secure a good future of our own making. Savoring these promises will satisfy the hungriest heart.

Wisdom and Justice

The mouth of the righteous utters wisdom, and his tongue speaks justice. The law of his God is in his heart; so his steps do not slip. *Psalm 37:30-31* (NASB)

We are righteous as we commit our futures to all that God is for us in Jesus, as he secures God's blessing and as he teaches us how to live with each other. For it is right to trust the promises of God so much that we live in obedience to his instructions. Being righteous means we know God. For how could we trust someone we don't know? We know him to be wise, powerful, self-sufficient, gracious, and merciful — in other words, he is holy. We know he created so we can experience and appreciate the fullness of his glory — he is good. We know he decides to reward those who love or hate him — he is just. Then in our knowledge of him, we agree with him that his way is the way to live. So as we delight in God's instructions, we will speak wisely and justly. Our speech will be wise in that it will convey to our listeners God's prescription for happiness; it will be pure, gentle, peaceable, reasonable, merciful, constant, and sincere speech. We will communicate justice in that what we say will not work to deprive anyone of God's gifts. Rather it will affirm and sustain God's sovereign grace, causing the humble to hope and the poor to persevere.

> O Lord, you are a God of wisdom and power, righteousness and justice. Grant me the confidence and courage to stand with you and speak in accord with your character. Amen.

Wisdom and Justice

Good Days

> Who desires life, and loves length of days that you may see good? Keep your tongue from evil, and your lips from speaking deceit. *Psalm 34:12-13*

Dad's aphorism, "It doesn't matter so much what you say, but how you say it," is only partially true. *What* we say matters. It matters to God. It matters so much to God that he determines the amount of good we experience according to what we say. If we speak what is true and good to those we meet, then God will be pleased enough to extend our days and cause us to receive good from his hand. The threatening opposite of this promise is also true, so the one who fears the Lord will hang on to the promise. Thus God punishes liars because they stand against his order for his creation. Treacherous speech violates the order of God's world in that it attempts to move people away from God's perfect design for just and righteous behavior. Deceptive and evil speech doesn't just promote violence; it is violence — both to God and to other humans. So God judges every effort to cause people to fear us instead of him. But the Lord rewards us greatly if we arrange our words so they cohere with his desire to bring about good in our lives and the lives of those who hear us speak.

> Because your truth is forever, O Lord; because your plans will succeed; cause me to speak so others will see reality clearly and walk in the light as you do. Amen.

Promises for the Battle

Good Days

Guarded from Sin

+————+

I will guard my ways, that I may not sin with my tongue. I will guard my mouth as with a muzzle, while the wicked are in my presence. *Psalm 39:1* (NASB)

"Eternal vigilance is the price of freedom." This aphorism is as true in the context of our relationship with God, as it is in the context of human governance. Like a terrorist, sin is sneaky. It creeps up on us and attacks from ambush. So we must constantly guard how we live. In particular we must guard our mouths, for they seem to be more troublesome than any other part of our anatomy. One or two words, spoken in the wrong way, at the wrong time, to the wrong person, can cripple us spiritually, making us even more susceptible to evil influences. Putting a moral muzzle on our own mouths is not easy, especially when we are around others whose speech is full of ungodliness, but it is necessary. The muzzle can take the shape of a commitment never to say anything, in any way, that dishonors God. Another way to prevent evil from coming out of our mouths is by filling our mouths with God's truth. Just as it is hard to speak clearly when our mouths are full of food, so it is difficult to speak evil, when our mouths are full of the love of God. We block evil from escaping by feasting on the truth of Scripture.

> "Set a guard, O Eternal, over my mouth. Keep watch over the door of my lips." May my mouth be compelled by your goodness and love.

Guarded from Sin

Approved Speech

The mouth speaks out of that which fills the heart. The good man out of his good treasure brings forth what is good; and the evil man out of his evil treasure brings forth what is evil. ... By your words you shall be justified, and by your words you shall be condemned. *Matthew 12:35-37*

When we stand before the Lord to hear his judgment concerning our lives on earth, we want to hear him say, "You are righteous." One way to be sure we will hear this is to talk properly. If good things come out of our mouths, a good verdict will issue from God's. What kind of words does God deem worthy of his approval? Words that indicate how much we treasure him. For our hearts to be full of good, as Jesus teaches, they must be full of God. When we love God with our whole heart, our speech will be useful, in that it will accord with his design for his creation. It will be righteous speech in God's ears. We will speak well of him, which will cause others to worship him. We will tell of his wonderful works, which will cause others to call on him. We will speak of his forgiveness, which will cause others to repent and return to him. We will talk of his faithfulness and righteousness, which will cause others to commit their futures to him. Then from him we will hear, "Well done!"

> Fill me with your Spirit — the fullness of your joy — so I bubble over with the memory of your abundant goodness, and sing joyfully of your righteousness, in Jesus' name. Amen.

Promises for the Battle

Approved Speech

Self-Preserving Speech

Laying aside falsehood, speak truth, to one another, for we are members of one another. ... Let no rotten word proceed from your mouth, but only such as is good for edification, according to the need of the moment, that it may give grace to those who hear. Ephesians 4:25 & 29

God has so constructed the Body of Christ in particular, and every organization in general, that how we talk to others affects our own well-being. We are not just members *with* one another; we are members *of* one another. He means this to be a powerful aid in our battle to control our tongues: We do not just hurt someone else when we speak deceitfully. We do not just help someone else when we speak decently. Because we are intimately connected to one another, our speech directly affects the speaker also. When we are gracious in our speech, everyone who hears benefits. Since we hear our own talk, we are among those who benefit. When we sensitively attempt to strengthen the faith of brothers and sisters in Christ in their moment of need, the words we hear coming from us strengthen our own faith as well. "From the fruit of a man's mouth he enjoys good, ... The one who guards his mouth preserves his life." God's grace extended in love envelops the giver and the receiver. Good news works both ways.

> Creative Lord, may my speech be rooted in your loving grace, so that the fruit of my lips tastes of Heaven and nourishes every heart it touches, including mine. Amen.

Self-Preserving Speech

Persuasively Sweet

The heart of the wise teaches his mouth, and adds persuasiveness to his lips. Pleasant words are a honeycomb, sweet to the soul and healing to the bones.
Proverbs 16:22-24 (NASB)

Godly wisdom is the ability to see what will bring us the greatest happiness for the longest time. So it's no surprise when Proverbs, the Bible's biggest repository of teaching about wisdom, repeatedly promises good to us if we will control our mouths. And it's no surprise that God appeals to our twin desires for personal pleasure and effectiveness to motivate us to employ our wisdom in controlling our speech. A well-taught mouth is clearly advantageous. It's also hard work. By nature our mouths are foolish and ignorant. We must strive to deliver sweet morsels with our tongues, morsels that change our hearers for good. Such discipline is a conscious effort; it doesn't happen by accident. Nor does it occur immediately or perfectly. We must be patient and persistent. We must become aware of the effect our words have on our hearers, and in what situations we tend to experience the most difficulty. Then we'll be able to say with Jesus: "The Eternal Lord has taught my tongue, so I may know how to sustain the weary one with a word."

> May the meditations of my heart and the words of my mouth be acceptable to you, O Lord, and change the lives of your people, in Jesus' name. Amen

Persuasively Sweet

Irreproachable Communication

+———+

Communicate sound ideas irreproachably, in order that the opponent may be put to shame, having nothing bad to say about us. *Titus 2:8*

Jesus doesn't call us to speak harshly or hatefully or haughtily either when we contend for the faith or when we are arguing for any other purpose. He asks us to be earnest and enthusiastic and empathetic. Since love should be the ultimate goal of our persuasion, then the way we reason must model that love, especially the manner of our speech. Even if we are reproached or reviled for what we say, we can — trusting in the God who judges justly — refrain from reviling in return; Jesus did. And he is the one we represent. It is worth every effort on our part to keep his name from being assailed. Therefore we can be free of guilt in our interactions with unbelievers, because we can learn to talk meekly, honestly, accurately, and courageously. We can be full of hope in these same conversations because, if we leave any possible opponents no room for reproach about the *manner* of our communication, God has less to overcome as they consider the *matter* of what we say. In other words, God may "grant them repentance that leads to an apprehension of the truth."

> Gentle Master, help me remember your Good Friday experience, so I will know it is possible to return a soft answer to harsh accusations, so the renewing power of your grace will be evident in every discussion. Amen.

Irreproachable Communication

Controlled for Praise

O Eternal, who may abide in your tent? Who may dwell on your holy hill? Those who walk with integrity, work righteousness, and speak truth in their hearts. They do not slander with their tongue, nor do evil to a neighbor, nor take up a reproach against a friend. *Psalm 15:1-3*

Fellowship with you is most precious, O God. There is no better place to be than in your presence; no better activity than engaging in conversation about you with others who love your glory. I will magnify your grace, rehearsing countless times my experience of the overflow of your joy. I will applaud your wisdom and extol your power. For you have used these not only to maintain yourself as a God worthy of worship, but also to work in my life since the day of my conception. To have fellowship with you, Father, is to delight in you as the Son does, to agree with your purpose as the Son does, and to extend your goodness as the Son does. It is worthy of all my love, loyalty, confidence, patience, and effort. I would rather be with you, humbly receiving gifts from your hand, than experiencing the short-lived thrill of self-exaltation that comes from maligning and defaming those around me. No self-created position of prominence compares with the glory of walking side by side with the Creator of the Universe. Controlling my tongue in my human relationships now is a small price to pay for the pleasure of knowing and praising your glory forever, through Jesus my Lord.

Controlled for Praise

About the Author

Doug Knighton has served as a chaplain in the United States Air Force Reserves since 1983. Before that he was an airborne, Ranger qualified Armor officer from 1969-73. As an active participant in military conflicts from Vietnam to Operations ENDURING FREEDOM and IRAQI FREEDOM, he has demonstrated a remarkable ability to address Scripture to the spiritual needs of his comrades in arms.

During 15 years of ministry to the men and women of the 434th Air Refueling Wing, he began to write short meditations on passages from the Bible that were appropriate for personnel who were deploying for service around the world. The first editions of "Promises for the Battle" were printed on post-cards and given to the men and women as they endured the departure process necessary for every deployment. Gradually they were collected and placed on the Wing's web page. During several post 9/11 assignments he discovered a way to use email to disseminate this material to a wide ranging audience of grateful readers.

Chaplain Knighton has been married to Maja for over 28 years. Together they have raised three children: Morgan, Charissa and Charlynn. He is an ordained minister in the

Conservative Congregational Christian Conference (CCCC) and has worked in a variety of ministries throughout his career, including ten years as a pastor to medical students and doctors associated with the Christian Medical & Dental Associations.

Scripture Index

Genesis 1:31; 2:3 26

Genesis 22:8, 13-14 164

Genesis 50:19-21 84

Exodus 14:13-14 156

Leviticus 19:19 98

Joshua 1:8 16

1 Samuel 23:15-17 158

2 Chronicles 20:14-15 160

Psalm 15:1-2 32

Psalm 15:1-3 188

Psalm 33:16-18 12

Psalm 34:12-13	176
Psalm 37:1-4	72
Psalm 37:6	152
Psalm 37:6-8	4
Psalm 37:30-31	174
Psalm 39:1	178
Psalm 78:69-72	44
Psalm 94:17-19	80
Psalm 121:1-8	58
Psalm 145:4-6	134
Psalm 145:18-20	54
Ecclesiastes 7:8-9	138
Ecclesiastes 10:10	24
Proverbs 10:9	34
Proverbs 16:22-24	184
Isaiah 41:10, 14	76

Jeremiah 17:7-8 70

Jeremiah 32:17, 27 170

Lamentations 3:24-25 148

Habakkuk 2:2-3 140

Habakkuk 2:13-14 166

Matthew 6:24, 33 30

Matthew 6:24-34 78

Matthew 12:35-37 180

Matthew 18:35 90

Luke 8:14-15 38

Luke 17:3-4 96

John 4:32-34 168

John 8:31-36 104

John 13:4-8 18

John 16:33 74

Acts 13:38-39 106

Romans 5:3-4 48

Romans 6:11-12 122

Romans 6:17-18 116

Romans 8:31-32 108

1 Corinthians 9:18-19 114

1 Corinthians 10:12-13 60

1 Corinthians 13:4 142

2 Corinthians 1:8-10 162

2 Corinthians 3:17-18 112

2 Corinthians 10:3-5 126

Galatians 5:1, 13 102

Galatians 6:8-9 50

Ephesians 4:12-13 36

Ephesians 4:25, 29 182

Ephesians 4:31-32 86

Philippians 1:6-10 20

Philippians 1:25-26 14

Philippians 2:12-13 56

Philippians 4:6-7 66

Philippians 4:8 120

Philippians 4:12-13 22

Colossians 1:9-11 146

1 Timothy 1:15-16................................... 150

2 Timothy 2:3-5... 40

2 Timothy 2:7.. 132

Titus 2:8 186

Hebrews 4:15-16.. 52

Hebrews 11:17-19.................................... 124

Hebrews 12:2-3.. 128

Hebrews 12:15 88

Hebrews 13:5 110

James 1:2-4 130

James 5:8-11 144

1 Peter 1:3-5 62

1 Peter 2:21-23 92

1 Peter 5:6-7 68

1 John 1:6-7 42

LaVergne, TN USA
30 December 2009
168516LV00001B/2/A